The Manly Art of Knitting

The Manly Art

Photography by MARLENE NORDSTROM DASSETT

of Knitting

by Dave Fougner

Published by **GINGKO PRESS**

Published in the United States of America, 2014
Second Printing, September 2016
Gingko Press, Inc.
1321 Fifth Street
Berkeley, CA 94710, USA
www.gingkopress.com

ISBN: 978-1-58423-556-9
LCCN: 2014941035

Printed in China

An edition of this work was originally published by
Threshold in 1972; it is with great pleasure that we
bring it back into print more than 40 years later.

FOREWORD

There is definitely a dual purpose in the writing of this book. The first is to introduce knitting to those men who have an interest but are reluctant to try. Then too, it is hoped that the many men who now knit will become less reluctant to admit it.

For those of you who are new to knitting, it is recommended that you read quickly through the book before starting any actual work.

CONTENTS

Basics

Pattern Stitches

Projects

Problems

Basics

A BRIEF HISTORY

Knitting apparently originated with the nomadic peoples of the Middle East. The knitting craft was spread by Arabic traders who taught the craft to sailors, as well as others who visited North Africa. When these men returned to Europe they taught the art of knitting to other men as well as women.

As knitting grew in importance, knitting guilds were established. If a man of that period was to become a Master knitter, he had to put in six years as an apprentice. After this the apprentice was tested to see if he had gained the expected proficiency. It was well worth the time spent. An accomplished knitter could win the favor of kings and queens.

As late as the 19th century it was common to see men knitting. But, as the importance of hand knitting declined and factory made clothing became available, knitting became the evening pastime of women. Men were forced through economic necessity to turn their skills away from knitting.

NEEDLE SIZE

Needles are numbered according to size. The smaller the
number the smaller the needle. It should be noted that if you
desire to make a blanket three feet wide and six feet long, the
larger the needle size, the fewer the stitches and therefore
the shorter the completion time. If you like to see results in
a fairly short period of time, use large needles. The beginner
should definitely use at least a size ten needle on his first
several projects.

YARN SIZE

Yarn, like needles, comes in several sizes, from the very
fine to the extremely coarse. Smooth and bumpy, nylon and
wool, inexpensive and expensive—yarns do vary. For your
first few projects, a thick yarn (rug yarn, Reynolds Lopi or 4
ply knitting worsted) is recommended. After this, experimen-
tation and instructions will guide you to the yarn best suited
to a particular project.

When you begin working on projects requiring several
bundles or skeins of the same color, yarn dye lot numbers
become important. Printed on each skein of yarn is a dye
lot number which indicates that the yarn will be the same
color as another skein with the same number. Buy more
than enough yarn the first time to finish the project.

CAST ON

The term "cast on" has characteristically been used for beginning, or placing the first stitches on the needle. This can be thought of as a series of knots. Tie a slipknot on to one needle.

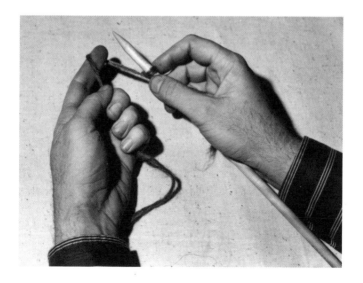

After this knot is secure, count it as the first stitch and make a knot similar to a half hitch for each additional stitch desired. To make the second knot, hold the needle in your right hand and the yarn in your left hand, palm up and point your left index finger. The yarn should be going over the top of this extended finger.

Twist your left hand toward you causing the yarn to make a loop around your finger.

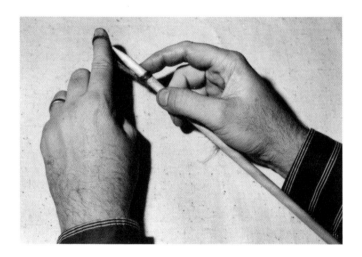

Using the needle, come up from behind the loop and push the stitch off your finger and on to the needle. Repeat this procedure for as many stitches as are required by the pattern.

THE KNIT STITCH

There are only two basic stitches in knitting. The Knit stitch is one which is used much of the time, and so must be mastered early.

After having cast on the desired number of stitches, place the needle with the stitches on it in your left hand. Hold the empty needle in your right hand with the yarn going through your right hand. Rest the end of the right needle in your lap. Hold the left needle in front so that the needles form about a 90° angle.

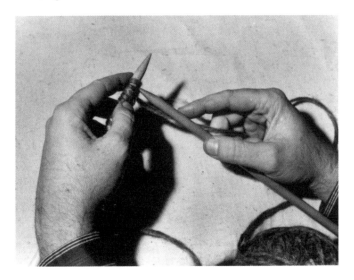

With the right needle, come from behind the first stitch and push the needle through the first stitch and under the left needle.

Using your right hand, take the yarn under and around the right needle.

Now bring the right needle back under the left needle.

Staying behind the stitch on the left needle, push the right needle over the left needle and push the stitch on the left needle off. Repeat as necessary.

THE PURL STITCH

The other principle stitch used in knitting is called the Purl stitch. Begin this in the same position as the Knit stitch (needles with stitches in left hand, empty needle in right hand, yarn through right hand, needles forming a 90° angle.)

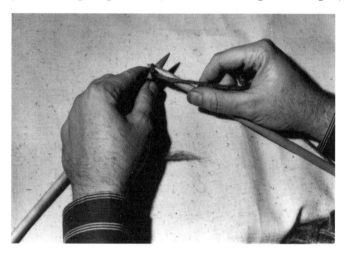

Coming from the front with the right needle, go through the first stitch and over the left needle.

Bring the yarn over and around the right needle.

Bring the right needle back and then push it under the left needle.

Pull the right needle to the right, slipping the stitch off the left needle. Repeat as necessary.

INCREASING

In some projects it may become necessary to add or increase a stitch. If you are Purling and must increase, take the yarn in your left hand and cast on one stitch.

If you are Knitting and must increase, move the right needle into the left hand and, using your right index finger, cast on one stitch.

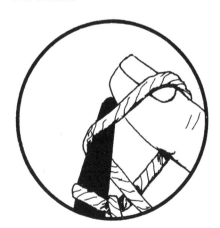

DECREASING
(Knit Two Together)

In working on different projects you will see the instruction, "K 2 tog." This means that you must treat two stitches on your left needle as though they were one. Coming from behind the two stitches, go through both with your right needle, and Knit as though they were only a single stitch.

This serves to reduce the number of stitches by one and may be used several times on any one row as indicated in your project instructions.

Some patterns may require knitting more than two together at one time. If your instructions say "K 3 tog" or "K 4 tog," you must Knit together the number of stitches listed as though they were only a single stitch.

YARN OVER

While knitting across a row the instructions may say "Y.O." or "O." This is accomplished by taking the yarn under the right needle and then over the top of the right needle.

This adds a stitch and creates a planned hole in your project.

This type of maneuver is normally found in projects which have a lacy effect. The beginner should be cautioned against starting out on a project with a lacy effect and wait until he feels extremely comfortable with the basic Knit and Purl stitches.

SL., P.S.S.O.

Part of what discourages would-be knitters from start-ing to knit is the seemingly foreign language often found in project instructions. The sl., or slip stitch, and the p.s.s.o., or pass slip stitch over, are usually used in projects which have planned holes in them for a fish net effect. To slip a stitch, place the right needle through the stitch on the left needle and slide the stitch onto the right needle. This is followed by Knitting the next stitch.

Then to p.s.s.o., using the left needle, lift up the slipped stitch on the right needle and pull it over the stitch that you just Knitted, then push it over the point of the right needle and let it fall there.

This reduces the number of stitches on that row. A similar effect can be created by Knitting stitches together. This latter method is usually easier for the beginner.

BINDING OFF

The time will come when pattern directions indicate that you should bind off all, or a certain number of stitches. This is accomplished by first Knitting two stitches.

Then lift the first stitch that you Knitted back over the second stitch and over the point of the right needle and let it fall there so that only one stitch remains on the needle.

Knit one more stitch and again lift the previously knitted stitch over this new stitch and over the point of the needle so that only one stitch remains on the right needle. The lifting process is normally preformed by the left needle and is continued until the necessary number of stitches have been bound off. When you are binding off the entire knit piece and you have only one stitch left on the needle, cut the yarn about five inches from the stitch. Slip the stitch off the needle and put the yarn through the stitch then pull gently to close the stitch. Weave this short piece of yarn into the back of the project using a crotchet hook.

GAUGE

Gauge can be especially important when you are working on projects where size is of concern. If you are making a ski sweater for yourself, and plan on the sweater being a size 46, then inches become crucial. The directions for most projects specify the gauge and list the type of yarn and needle size. The gauge tells how many stitches the knitter should have per inch.

To check your gauge before embarking on a project, knit about a 4" by 4" piece with the suggested yarn and needle size. Pick a row in the center where the stitches are not under any stress. Count the number of stitches in one inch. If the number of stitches is greater than the suggested number, there is a strong probability that your knitting is tighter than average. You should try a larger needle. The reverse is then true if you find yourself with fewer stitches per inch. Try a smaller needle. It is also possible that until you develop a consistent style of knitting, your gauge may change as you progress in your project. Check it occasionally.

BLOCKING

Blocking is done when size and fit are especially important. This is accomplished by stretching the project to the desired size (usually on a board), pinning it with stainless rustproof pins, pressing it with an iron through a damp cloth, and allowing it to dry. Many cleaning establishments are quite proficient at blocking, and unless you feel especially talented with an iron, blocking important projects is best left to them.

PUTTING THINGS TOGETHER

One of the easiest ways to put knitted pieces together is to use a crochet hook and weave the pieces together. Arrange the item to be put together as it would be if it were inside out. Using the crochet hook and a piece of yarn left over from the project, weave the yarn through the stitches at the edges of the project. If the pieces to be put together are over two feet long, it is best to tie a piece of yarn through the ends and the middle before beginning to weave it together.

Pattern Stitches

32

GARTER

The Knit and Purl stitches can be combined in many ways to give a variety of pattern stitches. Each pattern stitch has its own unique characteristics. Some are stretchy, some are solid and bulky, some are bumpy.

The Garter pattern gives a bumpy horizontal ribbed effect. It is accomplished by Knitting across every row.

STOCKINETTE

The most commonly seen pattern is called Stockinette. This pattern is created by using the Knit stitch for an entire row and then using the Purl stick for the next row. By alternating the Knit and Purl rows a smooth effect is created. The Stockinette pattern lends itself particularly well to such things as multi-color afghans and ski sweaters.

PURL

This is the reverse side of the Stockinette piece shown on page 35. The smoother Stockinette is most commonly used for the outside of garments. Sometimes, for unusual effects, the purl side is used for the outside.

RIB

This vertical ribbed effect can be accomplished by Knitting one stitch and Purling the next stitch across an entire row. The width of the Rib can be changed by Knitting two or more stitches and then Purling two or more stitches across the row. After you finish a row and start back, it should be remembered that any stitches you Knitted on the way over should be Purled on the way back, and any Purled stitch should be Knitted. After you Knit a stitch you must move the yarn under the front of the needle to be able to Purl the next stitch, and after you Purl a stitch you must move the yarn back under the front of the right needle to be able to Knit the next stitch.

Ribbing is stretchy and is used for necklines, cuffs and socks. Ribbing is not usually blocked because this would permanently flatten it out and its stretch would be lost.

MOSS

The Moss pattern, sometimes called "seed," is accomplished much like the Rib, but with a very different effect. As in the Rib, you knit one, Purl one, across every row. The important difference in the Moss pattern is that you must have an odd number of stitches (27, 53, 85 etc.) per row. This changes the placement of the stitches, and a bumpy effect instead of a vertical Rib will appear.

RICE

Another pattern which combines the Knit and Purl stitches is called Rice. After casting on the desired number of stitches, Knit all the way across the first row. On the next row you must Knit one, Purl one, Knit one, Purl one, all the way across. These two rows are then repeated throughout the pattern.

BASKET WEAVE

A woven effect can be created by the following method:

Row 1: Purl six, Knit two, repeat this across the row, ending with Purl six.

Row 2: Knit six, Purl two, repeat this across the row, ending with Knit six.

Row 3: Repeat row 1

Row 4: Knit two, Purl two, Knit six, repeat Purl two, Knit
six across the row, ending with Knit two.

Row 5: Purl two, Knit two, Purl six, repeat Knit two, Purl
six across the row, ending with Purl two.

Row 6: Repeat row 4.

Continue by repeating these six rows.

Projects

MAN'S BEST FRIEND

To get the feel of needles and yarn, you should start by knitting something for someone uncritical. Your dog won't mind a small blanket with an irregular shape and unusual stitches. Many people stop knitting before they start, disappointed by their first project's lack of perfection. Just as when you first started to use a hammer, you hit your thumb, when you first start to knit you will make mistakes.

Using size 13 needles and heavy rug yarn, cast on 50 stitches for a small dog, 75 stitches for a medium dog, or 100 stitches for a large dog. Work in the Garter pattern (that is, Knit every row) until you feel it is long enough for your dog. Bind off, and weave in yarn ends.

RIBBED CAP

A simple cap can be made by knitting a small rectangular piece.

Using size 13 needles, and Reynolds Lopi yarn, cast on 58 stitches. Work in the Rib pattern (Knit one, Purl one, across every row). When the piece is 12" long, bind off and weave in ends of yarn.

To finish the cap, place the piece down with the side you wish to be on the outside facing you. Pick up one end and fold it over the other end. Using a crotchet hook and a 1½ foot piece of the same type of yarn used to knit the piece, weave the yarn together through the stitches along the edge until the ends are woven together forming a tube. Weave another piece of yarn through the top of the cap. Pull the ends of this last piece of yarn together like a draw string, and tie them together tightly. Turn it right side out and fold up about 1½ inches for a brim.

50

WALL HANGING

This project makes a good background for display purposes and will give you practice in using different size needles and a variety of pattern stitches. You can use any size yarn with good results, but thick yarn will make a larger wall hanging.

Begin by casting on 23 stitches on size 15 needles, then work in the Moss pattern (page 40) until you have a four inch length of material.

Hold the needle with all of the stitches on it in your left hand, and take a size 10 needle in your right hand and use it to Knit together the first two stitches of the row. Continue using the size 10 needle and Purl the next stitch, then Knit one, Purl one for the remainder of the row. Exchange the size 15 needle for a second size 10 needle and work in the Rib pattern (page 38) until 4 more inches of the piece are completed.

With all the stitches on the size 10 needle held in your left hand, take a size 4 needle in your right hand and use it to Knit all the way across the row. Pick up your other size 4 needle and use the pair to work in the Rice pattern (page 42) for another 4 inches of material.

With all the stitches on the size 4 needle held in your left hand, take a size 15 needle in your right hand and Knit across the row. Pick up your other size 15 needle and use the pair to work in the Garter pattern (page 32) for another 4 inches of material.

Determine now which side is the best side of your work. This side should be facing you when you hold the size 15 needle with all the stitches on it in your left hand. If it does not, simply Knit an additional row, then pick up a size 10 needle in your right hand and use it to Knit across the row. Continue working in the Stockinette pattern (page 34) for 4 inches of material. End with a Purl row.

With all the stitches on the size 10 needle held in your left hand, take a size 4 needle in your right hand and Purl six, Knit two, repeating this across the row, and ending with Purl six. Pick up your other size 4 needle and use the pair to continue in the Basket Weave pattern (page 44) for 4 more inches of material.

With all the stitches on the size 4 needle held in your *right* hand, cast on one additional stitch, then transfer the needle to your left hand. Take a size 15 needle in your right hand, and Knit one, Purl one across the row. Pick up your other size 15 needle and use the pair to work in the Moss pattern for 4 inches. Bind off, weave in yarn ends, and block the piece so that it will lie flat against the wall when it is used.

YOUR HORSE IS NEXT
(The latest in circular knitting)

If you have been meaning to replace that leaky hose in the backyard, now is the time to do it. Cut a 40" piece of the hose and sharpen each end. This piece will be your circular needle. In circular knitting you Knit the first stitch cast, rather than the last cast (as you would if you were using two needles), and then you Knit around and around, making a seamless circle.

Passado's Pay Day—Cal-Western Appaloosa Hackamore Champion

Cast on 90 stitches of "Jumbo" yarn. Knit the first stitch that you cast and continue to Knit around and around until the piece measures about 32 inches long. Bind off, and weave in the yarn ends. You now have a saddle blanket (use it over a saddle pad).

If you don't have a horse, this project will make a good throw rug. Weave the edges together and block.

SLIPOVER

This sweater is simple to make. Two rectangles are joined at the sides and top, with openings for the arms and neck. It can be made in any size.

Measure the distance around the chest of the person for whom the sweater is intended. Be sure to measure at the fullest part. Using size 10 needles, knit a sample piece approximately 4 inches square. Check the gauge of this piece (page 26) to determine the number of stitches per inch. Multiply the number of stitches per inch by the number of inches around the person's chest. Divide the total by 2 to find the number of stitches needed for each half of the sweater. There must be an odd number of stitches for each half, so if you have an even number, add one stitch.

Using size 10 needles, cast on the correct number of stitches for one half of the sweater, and work in the Moss pattern. Hold the knitted piece up to the person to determine how long it needs to be. Bind off when it is long enough. Make the second half exactly the same as the first. Join the pieces at the sides and shoulders, then block the sweater.

ROPE HAMMOCK

Now that you have knitted something for everyone else, it is time to knit something for yourself.

Using shovel handles, or pool cues for needles (anything with a diameter of 1¼" to 1½") cast on 17 stitches using ¼" manila rope. Work in the Stockinette pattern until it is a little longer than you are tall. Bind off and weave in ends. Work large dowels through stitches at both ends and tie on ropes for hanging. Now your hammock is ready to be tied to your favorite trees. Relax and enjoy!

Problems

58

DON'T PUT IT DOWN

Until knitting becomes a habit you may have difficulty remembering whether to Knit or Purl after having set the needles down for a short time. When you are working with the Stockinette pattern this is a fairly simple problem. Pick up the needles as if to work. If the smooth side faces you it is time to Knit. If the bumpy side faces you it is time to Purl.

The problem becomes slightly more difficult if you are working with alternating Knit and Purl stitches. Pick up the needles as if to work. If the yarn coming from the last stitch comes naturally from the side facing you, then you have Purled the last stitch. If the yarn comes naturally from the far side, then you have Knitted the last stitch.

It is easier to remember what to do next if you finish the row you are working on before putting your knitting project down.

SPLITTING STITCHES

One of the discouraging things that occurs frequently when learning to knit is the splitting of a stitch. Two stitches are made from one when the yarn is split by the needle. To prevent split stitches, make certain while knitting that the needle goes straight through the stitch and not through the strand of yarn.

If you do split a stitch, you can work backwards to that particular point and correct it. However, if the project does not require perfection, you can Knit two stitches together to compensate and continue on.

THAT FOREIGN LANGUAGE

Many knitting patterns have abbreviations which may appear to be a foreign language. When you see "K," it means Knit. "K4" means Knit four stitches. The letter "P" means Purl. The letters "tog" stand for together, as in Knit two together (K2 tog). When "sl" is indicated, you must slip a stitch. The letters "yo" or "o" stand for yarn over. "P.s.s.o." tells you to pass the slipped stitch over the Knit stitch (this is also indicated as "sl, K and pass"). The letters "dec" stand for decrease, "inc" for increase, and "st" for stitch.

Like any foreign language, not nearly so difficult once translated.

RUNNING OUT

When working on projects which will require more than one skein of yarn, try to plan ahead before you run out. If you see that you will be running out in the middle of the next row, stop at the edge of the row. Cut off all but three inches of the excess yarn. Tie this three inch piece to the new yarn and continue with your knitting.

It is easier to weave in yarn ends on the edges of a piece than to weave them in at the center where they might leave a bump.

DROPPED STITCHES

Just as your wife's stockings will sometimes run, your knitting can develop a run. This run will occur when a stitch slips off the end of the needle. When looking at your knitting it will appear as though a stitch is running down the piece. To repair it properly you must have the run column between the needles. If you did not notice the dropped stitch immediately, knit until the column is between the needles.

When working in the Stockinette pattern, picking up a dropped stitch is fairly easy. Place the piece with the smooth side facing you. Using a toothpick or a small needle pointed at both ends, go through the stitch at the bottom of the run.

A horizontal piece if yarn will be above this stitch. There will be one horizontal strand for each row that the stitch has run. Go under the horizontal piece of yarn nearest the toothpick. You will now have two stitches on the toothpick.

Pick up the bottom stitch and bring it over the other stitch and the end of the toothpick. You will now have one stitch on the toothpick.

Go under the next horizontal piece of yarn and pass the bottom stitch up and over. Continue in this manner until you are back to the top row. Slip the final stitch back on the needle.

If you are working in other than the Stockinette pattern, the process is quite similar. Determine which side will require a smooth stitch (Knit stitch) and work that stitch as above. If the next horizontal strand comes from a bumpy row (Purl stitch), turn the piece over and work that stitch as above.

BIBLIOGRAPHY

Groves, Silvia, *Needlework Tools and Accessories*, County Life Limted, London, 1966.

Phillips, Mary Walker, *Creative Knitting: A New Art Form*, Van Nostrand, Rheinhold Co., 1971

"*Archaeology*", September 1955, Grass, Milton N., "The Origins of the Art of Knitting."

"*Antiques*", April 1942, Lyman, Lila Parrish, "Knitting: A Little Known Field for Collectors."